150 Quick Questions to Get Your Kids Talking

MARY E. DeMUTH

HARVEST HOUSE PUBLISHERS

EUGENE, OREGON

Cover by Left Coast Design, Portland, Oregon

Cover photo © Juice Images / Corbis

Published in association with the literary agency of Alive Communications, Inc., 7680 Goddard Street, Ste #200, Colorado Springs, CO 80920. www.alivecommunications .com.

150 QUICK QUESTIONS TO GET YOUR KIDS TALKING
Copyright © 2011 by Mary E. DeMuth
Published by Harvest House Publishers
Eugene, Oregon 97402
www.harvesthousepublishers.com

ISBN 978-0-7369-3005-5

Printed in the United States of America

11 12 13 14 15 16 17 18 / BP-NI / 10 9 8 7 6 5 4 3 2 1

To Patrick, Sophie, Aidan, and Julia

I'm forever changed
because we shared a table together.

Acknowledgments

I'm grateful for the team at Harvest House, who wholeheartedly championed this book and who value the family. LaRae, thanks for loving this idea!

Thank you, prayer team, who pray through every book I write: Amy, Anita, Ariel, Ashley and George, Carla, Caroline, Cheramy, Colleen, Cyndi, Jeanne, D'Ann, Darren and Holly, Dena, Denise, Diane, Don, Dorian, Elaine, Erin, Esther, Ginger and JR, Heidi, Helen, Jeanne, Jen, Jim, Jody, Katy, Kevin and Renee, Lesley, Leslie, Lilli, Liz, Marcia, Marcus, Marilyn, Marion, Mary, MaryBeth, Michael and Renee, Nicole, Pam, Patrick, Paul, Paula, Phyllis, Rae, Rebekah, Rod, Sandi, Sarah, Shawna, Shelly, Stacey, Sue, Susan, Tiffany, Tim, Tina, TJ, Tosca, Tracy, and Twilla.

And to Jesus, who asked great questions, shared significant meals, and welcomed everyone to His table: *Thank You* is never quite enough. May this book make You smile.

Contents

Introduction: Adding Some Spice to Your Mealtime Conversations

I've tried nearly every parenting method on the market. Sometimes I've felt elated that I've nurtured my children the way God wanted me to. Other times I've worried that I didn't discipline correctly. I've been stern. I've been lax. I've wavered. I've showered with love. But none of those methods captured my children's hearts quite so much as something I'll call conversational parenting—the kind of parenting that requires engagement and discourse. If you ask my kids about our time alone together, they will inevitably say, "My mom asks a lot of questions."

That's why I'm passionate about the content of this book. It will help you get to know your child's heart and mind as you ask great questions. My hope is that these queries will serve as springboards to your own family-shaped questions and that they will spark genuine conversations with your kids, whether they're toddlers or teenagers.

How Did This Book Come About?

From early on, our family of five spent evenings around the dinner table examining our days. We each shared one high and one low, although often those highs and lows turned into two or three of each. I loved learning about my children's hearts and the feel of their days as we shared a meal together.

Only when I started conducting research for one of my parenting books did I discover we were practicing the art of *examen*—an ancient spiritual exercise best done at the end of the day. Ivy Beckwith, author of *Postmodern Children's Ministry*, explains:

> Participants talk together about those things that happened during the day that sapped their zeal and energy, also known as *desolations*. Then they talk about those things that happened during the day that encouraged them or gave them energy, also known as *consolations*. At the end of the time we talk to God about all these things, bringing God into the very center of the important events of our lives.[1]

So we shared our consolations and desolations. We

sifted. We shared our trials and triumphs. But as we did this, a strange staleness crept into our ritual. Like a bland meal of boiled potatoes and tasteless chicken, our conversation lacked spice. On a long drive from Colorado to Texas after a terrific family vacation, I had a sudden inspiration. I would create questions that we could answer, one each night—in addition to our tradition of sharing high and lows. Thinking of my kids, I typed questions, reveling in each one, anticipating how each child would respond. When we returned home, I formatted the questions, cut them into squares, and placed them in a box in the center of our table. Each night the kids took turns pulling out a question.

The result? No more bland conversations.

Our table became a lively place of bantering, of exchanging ideas, dreams, and regrets. The questions probed into areas I hadn't expected. My kids learned about their parents. We learned about our kids—all in a nonthreatening, easygoing way.

Why is conversation like this so important? Why do parents need to pay attention to their kids' hearts and seek to engage them?

In the midst of a rapidly changing culture that embraces the values of community and authenticity, I've realized that some of the top-down parenting methods didn't prepare my children to step outside our front door. It wouldn't work for me to be the only one talking. Simply telling my children what to believe or how to act did not necessarily help them navigate the real world. Welcoming my children's thoughts by asking questions and listening not only validates their worth but also reflects the way Jesus prepared His disciples for their journey. And we all want our kids to be prepared when they leave our homes on their own journeys.

Peripateo Parenting

Jesus demonstrated the beauty of a conversational approach to life when He walked along the road with His disciples, asking questions, listening, and telling stories. The common Greek word used for this walking around is *peripateo.* Jesus embodied this kind of spirituality as He journeyed down dusty paths encouraging His friends. *Peripateo* has two meanings, however. The other meaning connotes the manner in which we conduct our lives. The apostle Paul used this word frequently: "As a prisoner for the Lord, then, I urge you to live [*peripateo*] a life worthy of the calling you have received" (Ephesians 4:1). Conversational parenting encompasses both. We walk with our children, talking about life along the way, and we show them how to love Jesus by the way we walk.

What Does Conversational Parenting Look Like?

Walking with our children, demonstrating how to live a life for Jesus—these sound ideal, but what do they mean? What are some practical ways to engage our children?

Sharing Our Stories

In this ever-shifting culture, kids long for things that are real. And they yearn for authenticity in their homes most of all. How do we model authenticity? By sharing our stories. By asking children to pray alongside us as we consider the future. By admitting we don't always have all the answers. The questions in this book are intended not only to help you know your kids but also to help them know you, understand your journey, and hear your story.

When our family made the excruciating decision to leave France, where we were planting a church, our daughter Sophie had the most difficult time processing our choice. She cried. She railed against the decision. I didn't have any words that would satisfy her anger, so I let her vent. I tried not to give her pat answers. As she got angrier, I prayed. I felt God prod me to tell her one reason why we were headed back to the States. I sat her down and shared one of my personal struggles with living in France. When I finished, she cried.

"I'm so sorry, Mom. I didn't know you went through that." Giving her an age-appropriate snapshot of my heart in that moment quelled her anger. My authenticity turned our conversation around. And my story helped her understand.

Encouraging Our Children in Their Own Paths

Proverbs 22:6 says, "Train a child in the way he should go, and when he is old he will not turn from it." We often think of that verse this way: *I'll raise my child the way I think he should go.* But the Scripture says, "in the way *he* should go." Conversation opens our eyes to the way God is leading our children. Not a week goes by that I don't ask, "What are you going to be when you grow up?" Once, Julia responded, "I'm going to be a meat catcher."

"A meat catcher? What is that?" I asked.

She rolled her eyes as if everyone should know what a meat catcher does. "It's someone who catches meat and gives it to poor people." Julia scrounged pennies and nickels to collect money for disadvantaged kids in Africa. She toted a little box and made a sign. She recruited her friends to donate. Our conversation, along with a hefty dose of observation, helped me see Julia's heart. She just may spend her life helping the poor. My job as a conversational parent is to identify her strengths and passions, encourage the unique gifts God has given her, and help her reach her goals.

That's what's so exciting about this book, particularly the philosophical questions it poses. These questions help you see your child's reasoning and passion.

Sharing Relaxed Meals

As I mentioned earlier, we parent around the dinner table. That's where we share our stories, ask questions, and interact. Not everyone does this, but those who do swear by it.

My friends Phil and Laina Graf are raising their kids in Amsterdam. How do they help their children navigate everyday life in that dark city? By parenting while they eat. One evening they discussed an invitation their daughter received to spend a weekend with friends in another city—with no parental supervision.

"I knew what choice I wanted her to make," Laina said, "but instead of telling her, I chose to listen." While they ate their meal, they engaged in a frank talk about sex and drugs and unsupervised weekends. "If I told her no right at the beginning, I would have ended the conversation at that point. We long for our children to be able to create their own decision-making grid so they can establish their own healthy boundaries." A hearty discussion led to her daughter's decision not to go on the weekend trip and to a time of emotional closeness (and a good meal to boot!).

Demonstrating Humility

But isn't authority what's needed? Shouldn't we show kids who's boss? Establishing authority is important in the early years, but as our children grow up, they relate to us less as authorities and more as fellow pilgrims. And we fellow pilgrims stumble in life. Why not be honest about it?

If we can't share our foibles with our children, if we present ourselves as having everything together, how will our children know we actually need Jesus? A conversational parent apologizes when she loses her temper. She admits she doesn't know all the answers. She invites questions. Her humble admissions show her children that even parents fail, that children aren't the only ones who sin. When we demonstrate humility, we show children how to behave when they've wronged someone. And although admitting our failure is painful, it shows a child how to repair a broken relationship and rebuild trust.

Conversational parenting is a great way to connect deeply with our children, particularly if we practice *peripateo* spirituality—something reminiscent of Deuteronomy 6:6-7: "These commandments that I give you today are to be upon your hearts. Impress them on your children. Talk about them when you sit at home and when you walk along the road, when you lie down and when you get up." As we share our own stories, encourage our children in the way God has shaped them to go, discuss life around the dining table, and practice humility, we'll begin to see camaraderie in our homes. And by God's grace, we'll prepare our children to meet the challenges this postmodern culture will throw their way. And all because of good questions and great conversations.

How to Use This Book

I've divided this book into 10 chapters with 15 questions per chapter. You can approach your question asking in myriad ways. If your children struggle with their past choices, read through chapter 1 and then spend some time asking about what happened "Back Then." If they're grappling with who they want to be in the future, check out chapter 3, which deals with aspirations. If you'd like some simple interaction, jump over to chapter 4, where the questions focus on descriptions. If you're teaching life lessons and choices, flip to chapter 9, which is about actions. Or simply use the conversation starters in random order. Next to each question, we've provided a box you can check when you've used it.

I've also added a short reflection at the beginning

of each chapter—something God is teaching me or my family about the subject. I hope these stories will help you consider the many ways God works in your life and give you the courage to share your own stories with your kids. In the end, your transparency will bring honest conversation into your home.

Now, Have Fun!

This book contains life-changing, interactive questions. I sincerely hope that as you query your kids (whether you pull the questions out of a box at the table or whisper them to your children at night on their beds), you'll unpack more of their hearts, more of their dreams. And that your relationships with them will deepen every day because of the surprising interaction.

May these simple conversation starters spark a new-found intimacy in your family and initiate great talks. As you strive to be a conversational parent who embraces a *peripateo* way of life, pray that God would use the questions you ask to deepen every relationship in your home. Your family is the first unit of community your child will ever experience, so why not petition God to make your home irresistible?

Now, ask away!

BACK THEN

1

Back Then

We live as creatures of regret. Even our kids experience this. And sometimes looking back on the past can tether us to those regrets.

What does a life that is free from past regrets look like? I picture someone singing, dancing, jumping, elating. But it must be more than that. Freedom can happen in the mundane, can't it? Can we be free this very moment? Can we let go of the angry fists shaking in our imaginations? Can we speak the truth in love *to ourselves*?

I ran across this great quote by Oswald Chambers about freedom today: "Let the past sleep, but let it sleep on the bosom of Christ, and go out into the irresistible future with him."[2]

Oh, there is so much to let sleep on Jesus' sacred

chest. So much regret. So much sin. So much internal wrestling. So much worry. So much fear. So much self-directed anger. Can I let it sleep? Truly?

I want to because going into the future with Jesus is truly irresistible, as Chambers says. And we can't walk that anticipatory path if we're wallowing in the past, keeping it very much awake. Oswald says to let it sleep, to cease from conscious action.

We sometimes resuscitate those old memories, those words, those sneers, those afflictions. We burn them onto a DVD and slip them quietly into our mental players, watching scene by scene with morbid fascination.

O dear Jesus, free our families from the past. Help us to let the past sleep. To let go of the bully memories. To break the DVD in half. Lead us forward, always forward to the irresistible place where our freedom lies.

Remind your kids that regardless of what they bring up from the past as they answer these questions, no regret is so big that Jesus can't cover it. Encourage them to share openly. And if possible, spend some time in prayer after they share.

Q:

When was the last time you cried? What made you cry?

Q:

What purchase do you most regret? Why was it a waste of money? What do you wish you would've done with the money instead?

Q:

What is the bravest thing you've ever done?

Q:

What have you done in the last week that was kind to the environment? Did you pick up trash? Recycle? Take a shorter shower?

Q:

What was the most recent movie you watched that brought tears to your eyes? Describe the scene that affected you that way.

Q:

What was your favorite toy as a four-year-old? (If you don't remember, pick a different age.) Why? Do you still have it?

Q:

What is one thing you've lost that you really miss?

Q:

What was the happiest day of your life so far? Describe it.

Q:

Which of the homes you've lived in is your favorite? Why? (If you've never moved, describe a home you really like—perhaps a friend's, a relative's, or a home you've seen on TV.)

Q:

What's the worst movie you've ever seen? Why didn't you like it? What about the movie made you cringe?

Q:

When were you the most discouraged about school and grades?

Q:

What was your favorite television show (or DVD) from two years ago? Why? Recall one episode you really liked.

Q:

What was your most embarrassing moment?

Q:

What do you regret most about last year? What would you change if you could?

Q:

When was the last time you belly-laughed?
What was so funny?

THE BIG TODAY

2

The Big Today

I recently received a very encouraging e-mail from a friend. Her words still ring in my head, circling down into my heart and feeding my soul.

> We may now and then think of how God cleanses us from sin—our own sin. Less often do we consider that He cleanses us from the sin of others. Awfully good that He does both, in addition to providing the remedies for our guilt and for our weakness. I am certain that at best I only faintly grasp how comprehensive His salvation offer is.

God does indeed cleanse us from all sin. And I'm blessed and surprised when I think He cleanses us from the sin of others too. I read Genesis 50:20, where Joseph said his brothers intended to harm him, but God meant it for good. Maybe that's how God cleanses us from the sin of others in the Big Today. Joseph's brothers obviously sinned against him. But by God's grace, he chose to forgive. He'd been given so much of God's purpose and plan that he let go of the past pain in order to move forward in the moment. And as he did that, he was set free from bitterness.

Isn't that how it is with us? We'd rather hold on to the sin folks have thrown our way, nursing it, coddling it. We forget that God wants to wash that away from us, to set us free in the now of today. We hold on tightly to the painful words spoken over us, the hurtful acts done to us, forgetting that Jesus stands ready to take those words and acts upon Himself. But He can't take them if we smother them to ourselves.

Real freedom comes when Jesus cleanses us from all sin. And it comes when we give Him the sins others have committed against us. It's all a grand letting go, isn't it? But we must let go to have the freedom to move into the future joyfully.

As you ask your kids questions about the Big Today, keep in mind the importance of letting go of bitterness. Remember that the God who gave Joseph the grace to forgive is big enough to help your children navigate the pitfalls of school and life. He rejoices over our children (and us) with singing. He enables us to fully enjoy the beauty of today.

Q:

Why do some people tease others? What do you do when someone teases you? Or your friend?

❑

Q:

What are you most afraid of? Sickness? Monsters? Scary movies? Why?

❑

Q:

What is your favorite song? Why do you like it so much? If you have your MP3 player nearby, play it for the family.

Q:

What is one thing you wish you knew how to do really well?

Q:

How can you tell when someone is lying? Is it easy or hard for you to lie?

❏

Q:

What does good money management look like for you? Which do you like more, saving or spending? Why?

❏

Q:

What kinds of situations make you angriest? Why?

Q:

What is your favorite movie? Describe one scene you really liked.

Q:

What would your best friend say really gives you the creeps? Would he or she be right?

Q:

If you could purchase a car today, what kind would you like? What do you like about that kind of car?

Q:

What is the biggest waste of your time?

Q:

What food would you most like to learn how to cook?

Q:

How do you make friends? When is making friends easy for you? When is it hard?

❒

Q:

What frustrating habit would you most like to break?

❒

Q:

What is the one thing you wish you had this year that would make it the best ever?

ASPIRATIONS

3

Aspirations

I'm often aspirational as a parent, thinking of what I'd like to be in the future, rather than operational, thinking of how things will work today. This morning as I cleaned out our crisper, I located my aspirational carrots. When I saw them at the store a month ago, I said to myself, *Don't pay extra money for the little peeled carrots. Buy the cheaper carrots and peel them yourself.*

So I listened to my aspirational self and took the unpeeled carrots merrily home. The poor carrots sat languishing in the crisper all this time while convenient salad fixings made their way out into the real world of our kitchen and then our stomachs. When I found the carrots today, they were growing. Little carroty sprouts furred each one.

I laughed because this is so like me. I *aspire* to be the

thrifty shopper I was when we had very little money. I am still very thrifty. But the reality (the operational part of my life) is that little wee carrots without peels would actually get eaten because I don't have time to peel their longer, hairier counterparts.

How much of your life is aspirational? How much of your kids' lives is aspirational? You aspire to be an organized person, but operationally, your desk resembles my hairy carrots. You aspire to recycle your cans, but they sit guiltily in the bottom of your too-large waste bin.

Today I went to the store and bought three small bags of those wonderful little carrots. Lo and behold, they were on sale! Buying them showed me I'd grown up just a little bit. I recognized my busy life and chose to purchase something the family could enjoy now.

There's a lesson here for my walk with Jesus. I don't always evaluate myself accurately. I aspire to be a...

great mommy	productive writer
supportive wife	avid discipler
exercising guru	prayer lady
Bible devourer	organizing queen

But operationally I'm not all these things. I'm just plain ol' me, who struggles, falls down, and gets back up again. I throw away hairy carrots. I say words I regret. I occupy myself with the urgent and forget the important. That's where I am. My kids are the same way. They make grandiose plans to keep their rooms clean or memorize Bible verses, only to throw clothes willy-nilly on the floor or cram verses into their heads on the way to church.

And yet we can all be thankful because Jesus takes us at our operational level. Somehow, by His strength, He moves all of us toward His aspirations for us, and yet He accepts us today where we are and loves-loves-loves us here and now.

As you ask these future-oriented questions, remember my aspiratonal carrot lesson. We may talk big about what we hope to be, but only by the fascinating grace of God can we actually become what He endeavors for us. He is there in our hopes and in the gritty truth of today. Encourage your kids to dream in like manner, but also shower them with grace-infused encouragement when they opt for the peeled carrots of reality. We're all in process, with aspirations aplenty, failures in the present, and a God who cheers us in whatever place we find ourselves.

Q:

Describe the ideal spouse. (Parents: How would you have answered this question before you met your spouse?)

❏

Q:

Describe your dream house. How many rooms? Square feet? A pool? Acreage?

❏

Q:

What museum would you like to go to next year? Why?

Q:

How will you know when you've met the person you'll marry? (Parents: How did you know?)

Q:

What do you want to be when you grow up?
(Parents: What did you imagine you'd be when
you grew up?)

❏

Q:

When you grow up, would you rather live in the
country or in the city? Why?

❏

Q:

If you could plan a family fun day for this Saturday, what would we do? Describe the day, hour by hour.

Q:

If you could go to any college in the world, where would you go? Why?

Q:

If you could go anywhere on vacation this summer, where would you go?

Q:

If we had extra money this year, how would you like us to spend it?

Q:

Dream big: If you could have any pet in the world (with no limitations…even a shark!) what would it be? Why?

Q:

If you could work in any country of the world, what country would you choose? Why?

Q:

Describe your dream job.

Q:

What five things do you want to do before you die? (In other words, what is on your bucket list?)

Q:

What will you do with your kids that we do now as a family?

DESCRIBE…

4

Describe...

One of the coolest things about kids is their ability to observe something and then describe it. I admire that skill and try to coax it back into my life. As I consider the importance of remembering and describing, I'm reminded of a time way back when.

I didn't have great penmanship in high school. My pen-to-paper antics were inconsistent and haphazard—until I received a note from my new friend Kerry. She was a cool senior; I was a junior and new to that high school.

Her handwriting was stunning. Perfect print, perfectly spaced. It made me long to write beautifully. And so I practiced until I improved.

Every once in a while I slop my words across a page, only to remember Kerry's notes and beautiful penmanship. I stop. Pause. Then I slow down and write like Kerry. She probably doesn't know I admired this little trait in her, but I'm thankful for her example nonetheless.

Kerry's actions remind me today of how important other people's lives are to us. Of how deftly little kindnesses maneuver their way into our hearts. Of how much we need to slow down long enough to remember people—what they do, how they act, what they say. And Kerry's notes also remind me that others watch me. How am I creating beauty where I go? What in me makes others want to describe me? What part of Jesus seeps out of me, enticing others to follow Him?

All this comes from reflection. From being willing to stop, slow down, and watch life and the people in our lives. To observe and then describe.

Had I been excessively hurried in high school, I wouldn't have taken time to see the beauty of Kerry's handwriting. Her sweet notes opened up a door of friendship I needed. But what if I'd been too rushed?

If our families are too rushed, we won't spend time making beauty, cultivating it. Then no one will see. No one will have the opportunity to appreciate. No one will know our connectedness to the Creator.

Oh, to slow our families down. To appreciate the hollyhocks in the yard. To write a well-penned note. To revel in my daughter's singing voice. To encourage my kids to observe things, to take on the discipline of describing what they see and feel.

This life is too short to waste on worry and hurry. It's time we push the pause button long enough to listen to our kids (and ourselves) describe the world around us.

Q:

Describe what a day of genuine rest would look like to you.

Q:

Describe a time you were jealous of a friend. What happened? Why were you jealous?

Q:

Describe someone who has a beautiful soul.

Q:

Describe the stupidest commercial you've ever seen.

Q:

Describe a time in your life when you were very, very afraid.

Q:

Describe a teacher from last year. What did you enjoy about him or her? What bothered you?

Q:

Describe a popular classmate (parents: a well-liked coworker). Why do you think he or she is popular?

❏

Q:

Describe what you'd wear to the Academy Awards.

❏

Q:

Describe your scariest dream.

Q:

Describe the perfect friend. In what ways are you a good friend? What do you need to do to become a better friend?

Q:

Describe a bully you've known before. Did he or she ever hurt you or a friend of yours? Why do you think he or she behaved that way?

Q:

Describe your ideal vacation (if money was no object). Where would you go? What would you do? Who would be with you?

Q:

Describe your strangest dream.

Q:

Describe the best meal you can imagine. How many courses? What would you drink? What would you have for dessert?

Q:

Describe your meanest teacher.

RECOUNT OR LIST...

5

Recount or List...

Rarely does a gift knock me down, bless my socks off, and make me flat-out cry. But once, I received a book compiled by my friends George and Ashley, dear friends across the miles. They contacted as many of my friends as they could find and asked them to write me encouraging letters. Then they compiled the letters and bound them into a book. I spent my birthday crying tears of appreciation for all the varied and beautiful relationships in my life.

Why? Because the book felt like a warm embrace of Jesus, so much needed, so much appreciated. I was humbled as I read words from friends, encouraging words, uplifting words, life-giving words—lists of ways God has healed me and changed me and dared to use my life in the lives of others.

And as is often the case in my world, I had to fight my way through the book, straddling the line between joy and worry. Joy because I loved hearing that folks saw Jesus in me. (They mentioned that on nearly every page.) Worry because I didn't want to take all those kind words into my heart lest I become too focused on myself. He must increase; I must decrease.

And yet, by the time I was finished with the book, a deep sense of awe hung over and swirled through me. God saw fit to swoop from heaven, rescue me from my own pain, and set me free to love Him. No testimony on this earth is better than the simple telling of what Jesus does in each of our lives. The listing of His accomplishments. The recounting of what He has done...

He befriended me.	He hope-filled me.
He healed me.	He changed me.
He found me.	He remade me.
He settled me.	He rescued me.
He brought me home.	He loved me.
He sought me.	He loves me still.
He died for me.	

I may be an oldster to my kids (who can't fathom life after 30), but I am so young today—like a child skipping free. I can honestly say that God saw fit to change my life utterly. I am never the same. And I travel forward with hope and His presence.

Like David, I list what God has done. I recount His power. Consider David's pleas and God's promises in Psalm 40:1-5:

> I waited patiently for the LORD;
> he turned to me and heard my cry.
>
> He lifted me out of the slimy pit,
> out of the mud and mire;
> he set my feet on a rock
> and gave me a firm place to stand.
>
> He put a new song in my mouth,
> a hymn of praise to our God.
> Many will see and fear
> and put their trust in the LORD.
>
> Blessed is the man
> who makes the LORD his trust,
> who does not look to the proud,
> to those who turn aside to false gods.
>
> Many, O LORD my God,
> are the wonders you have done.
> The things you planned for us
> no one can recount to you;
> were I to speak and tell of them,
> they would be too many to declare.

Like David, we are called to examine our lives, to recount His faithfulness. My friends George and Ashley helped me trace the fingerprints of God through their outrageously beautiful gift, and we, as parents who love our kids, can do the same by asking great questions and then sitting back and actively listening to the lists our kids recount.

Q:

If you were stranded on a deserted island, what three things would you most want to have with you? Why?

Q:

Look back on your day. If you could change it, how would you? What would you keep the same?

Q:

What is your fondest summer memory? Who were you with? What were you doing? Where were you going?

Q:

What was the best thing that happened to you when you were five? (Change the age if another one works better.) The worst?

Q:

What was your favorite birthday present? Christmas present?

⬚

Q:

If you could have anyone over for dinner, who would it be and why? What would you want to eat for dinner? What questions would you ask your guest?

⬚

Q:

Interview the person on your left for a job. You choose the job and then ask five questions.

Q:

What five things would you do at the ocean if we went there today?

Q:

List as many states as you can as a family. Can you list the capitals too?

Q:

What four crops would you plant in a garden? Why those?

Q:

What toy did you want that you never received?
Do you still want it now?

Q:

List seven things you are thankful for today.

Q:

List five things you could give to a homeless person that would help him or her today. Why those things?

Q:

List five adjectives that describe you. Then list five adjectives to describe the person on your right.

Q:

What six things would you like to do in the mountains if we ventured there today?

PHILOSOPHICAL
QUESTIONS

6

Philosophical Questions

My children chatter about the meaning of life when food is placed in front of them. I'm not sure why, other than it's some sort of innate thing. Food in, words out. Here's a glimpse into our dinnertime conversation:

Aidan: "Hey mom, I talked to Jeremy today."

Me: "Oh really, what about?" I was curious since Jeremy had taken a liking to calling Aidan an idiot "and other bad words."

Aidan: "About God." He looked at Julia. "You remember how you asked him if he believed in God?"

She nodded.

"Well, I don't think he does. At lunch today he said that he doesn't pray. Doesn't read a Bible ever. Doesn't think God is real. He isn't a Christian."

"Maybe he's like the Ninevites," Julia said.

Patrick and I laughed. Perhaps they've watched too much Veggie Tales' *Jonah*!

Sophie said, "Yeah, I got in a God-talk today."

"Really?" I asked. "What about?"

"Well, we were discussing how the universe started and creation. One friend believes in evolution. Another believes that Adam and Eve and Eden happened, but in the middle of the dinosaur era, after the Big Bang. I told them what I believed."

How old is *Sophie?* I wondered. I couldn't believe how nonchalant and bold she was. She just said it like it is. Told her friends without shame that she believed in God.

Sophie continued. "The girl who believes in the Big Bang *and* God believes she will go to heaven. But once she's there, she'll become something new, like a lizard. The other girl believes in heaven, sort of. She thinks that when she dies, she goes somewhere, and if her soul is not united to her body (she has to run around looking for it), she goes to hell. If it unites, she goes to heaven. Then another girl came into our discussion. I shared with them all about the book of Revelation and how someday we'll all be judged. The new girl, who at first said she was not a Christian, decided she was a believer after hearing me talk about Revelation. I guess she was scared."

Our children chat boldly about Jesus and engage in philosophical discussions both at school and around our dinner table. Though others may be like Ninevites (in Julia's vernacular), our kids dare to talk about the gospel plainly, with love and grace. When Jesus said to come to Him like a child, I picture Him pointing to my children.

As you seek to know the hearts of your kids through these philosophical questions, I pray you'll see hints of Jesus in their answers. And as you answer them yourself, may they see Him in you as well.

Q:

Do fame and money fill someone up all the way? Why or why not?

Q:

What does it mean to be in debt? Why is it hard for people to climb out of debt?

Q:

Why do crummy things happen to wonderful people?

Q:

What is gossip? Why is gossiping unwise?

Q:

Why are some people poor and others are rich? What can we do today to help those who are less fortunate than we are?

Q:

What are some reasons why some people take illegal drugs or drink too much alcohol? Why is quitting such habits so difficult?

Q:

What does the word *grace* mean to you?

Q:

Is driving faster than the speed limit always wrong? Why or why not?

Q:

Why is evil in the world? Can you do anything to stop it?

Q:

Why is it a trap to always want to be liked by everyone?

Q:

What does it mean to be real or authentic? Why do some people hide behind a mask instead of being themselves?

Q:

What is a budget? Why is sticking to a spending plan so difficult?

Q:

What does it mean to be addicted to something? What are some things people can be addicted to?

Q:

What is honesty? Dishonesty?

Q:

Is telling a lie ever okay? If so, when?

IF…

7

If...

If is a deeply creative word. It's full of possibilities. And adding *what* invites even more creativity. We changed the way we interacted with God as a family by simply asking, *What if we changed the meaning of quiet time?*

We used to shudder at the words *quiet time.* Those two words have unwittingly heaped loads of guilt upon our desire to connect with God. Because of those words, we've believed that to know God deeply, we had to adhere to a series of spiritual lists. Read the Bible like an instruction manual and dissect it. Pray, but not too much about ourselves. Spend at least an hour, and, of course, it must be at six in the morning, or it's not sanctified.

My friend Erin started a what-if revolution in my heart when she sent me a gift—one of her amazing art journals, full of small-scale art projects. She'd been going through a move, so she decided to create artistic responses on the pages of a five-by-seven journal as a reaction to all the changes she'd encountered. She cried out to God. She pasted house listings inside and wrote Scripture over them. She wondered if and how God would provide a home for her family. She painted some of the pages and highlighted key verses God breathed to her during the tumult.

This made sense. We could see how Erin was using her what-if creativity to connect to God in a personal way. As a family, we decided to do the same—on a less grand scale. The good news is that we didn't have to be budding artists to create a highly personal, deeply spiritual art response.

Not sure where to start?

- Start with a clean sheet of paper (or better yet, the blank side of a recycled page).

- Approach Bible reading like this: When a verse jumps out, have kids your write it down and add magazine pictures to illustrate it.

- Create a page just for prayers. On the left side list the date and the request, leaving the right side blank to record God's answer to your prayer.

- Write out what's bothering you. When I worried about how many hats I was wearing, I placed different hat stickers all over one page and listed the hats. Seeing them all visually helped me to realize I needed to trim down a few of my roles. My daughter Sophie had a similar collage full of too many tasks. It helped her to visualize how cluttered her life became.

Through this process of illustrating our quiet times, we realized we served and loved a creative God who designed the beauty of this earth with a word—and designed us to think about the what-if questions life threw our way. Ephesians 2:10 tells us that we're not only our Creator's masterpieces; we're designed in His image—to do creative works ourselves.

Connecting to God through art has revolutionized our family's time with Him—now it's full of surprises. We revel in discovering new Scriptures to illustrate in simple, stick-figured ways. We look forward to creatively responding to His words for us as we wait in expectancy for *His* creative ways to surprise us. And we're forever changed in the process.

You don't have to draw a picture or sing a song to be creative though. Simply bringing up the possiblity of doing things differently or posing a probing question awakens what-if thinking. And part of growing deeply as a family involves this kind of speculative thinking. Though you may not fancy yourself a creative type, enjoy these questions and delight in the answers your kids share.

Q:

If you could choose a nickname for yourself,
what would it be?

❏

Q:

If you could create something with your hands
and imagination, what would it be? Dream big!

❏

Q:

If you could live in any time period, which would you choose? Why?

Q:

If you had to work at a mall, what store or restaurant would you work in?

Q:

If you could travel to any planet, which one would you see? Why?

❑

Q:

If the calendar today said January 1, what would your New Year's resolution be?

❑

Q:

If you could change one thing about the world, what would it be?

Q:

If you could create a beautiful painting of anything, what would you paint? Why? Where would you display your painting? Would you sell it?

Q:

If you could be amazing at any sport, what would it be and why?

❏

Q:

If you could write a book that was guaranteed to be published and make money, what would it be about? What would the title be?

❏

Q:

If you had $5000 to give away today, whom would you give it to and why?

Q:

If you could collect anything, what would it be? Why?

Q:

If you could perform in any musical or play, which one would you choose? Why?

❒

Q:

If you could be one zoo animal, what would you be? Who would everyone else in the family be?

❒

Q:

If you could be any character from a book or movie, who would you be? Why that person?

ALL ABOUT OTHERS

8

All About Others

In a dream, I went to a doctor's office for insomnia. As sometimes happens in strange dreams, I had my nightgown on, and it kept slipping off. By the time I found the doctor in a serpentine series of rooms, I was a mess—crying, frightened, hyperventilating.

He tried to shove an oxygen tube up my nose. Then he asked the nurse to turn me over on an inclined board. He was convinced he knew why I wasn't sleeping. It had to do with my feet. He slowly started pushing long, thick needles into my heels. All the while, I panicked and wept. He was the last resort for figuring out my insomnia, but he seemed lost and incompetent. I woke up as he pushed one needle into my heel bone.

As I thought about the dream, I remembered one

of the lessons God has been teaching me: Regardless of what I may think, humans can't completely heal or fill us. I wish they could. And as I write this, I wish I could be that kind of human. We're all broken and needy and terribly incapable of loving well—even in our families, which are supposed to be havens. Sure, we may have brushes with brilliance, but the truth is, in every relationship, we will let others down, or others will let us down.

We often place our happiness in the hands of others, forgetting that Jesus is really the only one we can completely entrust ourselves to safely. And even He is not completely safe in one sense because He isn't after our happiness. He's after our holiness.

Jesus calls us to something higher. He would have us entrust ourselves to others in holy anticipation, yes, but we are to rest our well-being only in the One who created us. Ultimately, deep happiness comes when we run headlong into Jesus. He created us. He knows us.

People, even well-meaning folks, can never fix us and fill us the way Jesus can. No doctor, no best friend, no spouse, no parent, no child. I've been guilty of thinking that if all my relationships were stress free, I'd be happy. If everyone loved me the way I want to be loved, I'd be happy. But God calls us higher. Will I be happy if others don't fill me? Will I continue on if a friend betrays me? Will I be okay if my relationships go in different directions than I expect them to?

We must teach our kids these hard but freeing truths. That others may let us down, but God will shoulder the ache. That He will enable us all to love well, to forgive, to move forward. Though our relationships outside and within the family may shift, He is the ever constant One.

Q:

Paraphrase "love your enemies" without using the words *love* or *enemies*. Remember a time when you had to love an enemy. What happened? How did loving your enemy make you feel?

Q:

If you were at a fun party but didn't know anyone, how would you start a conversation with a stranger?

Q:

What was the best gift you've given to someone? Did he or she enjoy the gift?

Q:

When was the last time you said, "I'm sorry"? Describe the situation surrounding your apology.

Q:

If you could go on a date with your mom or dad, what would you do? Describe it.

Q:

If you could write a letter to anyone in the world and were guaranteed he or she would write back, who would you write? What would you say?

Q:

What do you think your parents' lives were like when they were your age?

Q:

How would your best friend describe you?

Q:

Describe what Dad and Mom do all day at work.

❏

Q:

How are you different from your mom and dad?

❏

Q:

Have you ever had a friend who seemed to become an enemy or traitor? What happened?

❏

Q:

What do you appreciate most about your parents? Grandparents? Cousins?

❏

Q:

Whom do you know who is shy? How can you help him or her come out of his or her shell?

Q:

What do you think bothers the person to your left the most? Why?

Q:

How are you similar to your mom and dad?

ACTIONS AND CHOICES

9

Actions and Choices

I sat at my keyboard in my office when I heard my daughter Sophie's voice behind me.

"Mommy?" she said.

"Yeah? What do you need?" I asked.

"Well, it's just that…You know how a lot of teen-age girls don't really like their moms?"

"Yes."

"I don't want us to be that way, Mommy. Because I really, really love you, and I can't imagine us being that way."

"I don't want to be that way either," I said. "What do you have in mind?"

"Can we spend time together? Just you and me? I really liked it when we made cards together. Can we do that more?"

I nodded. I'd been struggling lately to find good balance in my life. I worried that I hadn't connected enough with my children. Just like you, I wear many hats:

lover of Jesus	bill payer	teacher
wife	church planter	hostess
mommy	chef	errand runner
writer	gardener	
housekeeper	exerciser	

So I made a schedule. I blocked time for things like family movie night, exercise, making cards with Sophie, reading to my children. I posted it on the fridge for further accountability. As one who has in the past been enslaved to lists, I hesitated. I know how they can tyrannize me. Yet I also know that discipline in life brings great rewards. So I am swinging back toward discipline and making good choices for the sake of my kids because the truth is, my kids watch me. They observe how I order my life, how I choose what to do and when to do it. I'm the model. They pay attention to my actions.

And you know what? I'm enjoying my time with Sophie. I anticipate deeper conversations. Yesterday, as we gardened, we spoke unfettered words to each other—mother-daughter words about womanhood.

I am deeply humbled and excited by Sophie's voice

from behind me in my office. Hers was another reminder that the people God has placed in my life are far more important than mere tasks. My choices in life matter. My connection to my family matters. And my choice to interact with them deepens our community.

Some of the questions that follow are silly, some serious. Some are about important choices or decisions, and others are helpful fillers about ice cream flavors (which do you choose?) or what makes you laugh. Enjoy the variety as you explore a wide range of choices.

Q:

If you could change a choice you made in the last month, what would it be? What would you change?

Q:

Play truth-or-dare around the dinner table. Why did you choose truth? Or dare?

Q:

Ask the person on your right any question you choose.

Q:

Say one thing you admire about a choice that the person on your left has made.

Q:

A genie grants you three wishes. What do you wish for? (Sorry, you can't wish for more wishes!)

❏

Q:

Ask Mom or Dad any question you want about their childhoods.

❏

Q:

What's your favorite ice cream flavor? Before you say yours, first guess everyone else's.

Q:

Give an example of a famous person's wrong choices and how those choices changed his or her life.

Q:

Which is your favorite, sunrise or sunset? Why?

Q:

What is your favorite chore around the house? Why? What's your least favorite?

Q:

What makes you laugh (slapstick, jokes, goofy people…)? Choose as many scenarios as you can. (Extra credit if you make your family laugh!)

Q:

What would you like about being a carpenter? What would you dislike about it?

Q:

Do you think most Hollywood stars are happy?
Why or why not? Can you think of any wise
choices your favorite star has made? What are
some unwise choices?

❏

Q:

Which season of the year is your favorite? Why?

❏

Q:

What type of weather scares you the most?
Why?

YOU AND YOUR WORLD

10

You and Your World

My children are growing up. They're 18, 15, and 12 now, though I keenly remember diapering them and cooing over them as babies. I've realized as they've grown that my number one job, as my speaker friend Leslie is apt to say, is to work my way out of a job—to prepare them for the big, bad world.

As one who espouses that the first true, genuine, infectious community is the family, I believe that the way we demonstrate Jesus to our families in the midst of our changing world will have deep and lasting impact not only on our culture but also on the kingdom of God.

Our family spent two and a half years living in post-Christian France during our children's formative years. Through many tears and hard-won discussions, we learned to thrive. We honed our conversational parenting around the dinner table.

We try to have conversations that make our kids wildly enthusiastic about our home. We strive to create the kind of community that's haven-like—a place where kids aren't afraid to be themselves, where they're applauded for being comfortable in their own skin. This is not at the expense of engagement, nor is it embracing protectionism. This kind of authentic interaction not only benefits children and families but also, if taken to its logical conclusion, helps everyone in our communities of faith better interact with the world around us. Havens do that.

So, in the land of postmodernism on steroids, we watched our children experience redemption. Our eldest daughter led her atheist friend to Jesus after loving her, talking to her, and praying for her more than a year. Our son expressed his frustration to his friend's parents (in French) when they showed a demonic film for a birthday party. And our youngest daughter met Jesus in France. Her father baptized her in the Mediterranean Sea.

Bishop Whipple, known as the Apostle to the Indians, said this: "For the last thirty years, I have looked for the face of Christ in the people with whom I have disagreed." His words clearly expose the beauty of what I call the paradox of engagement and purity. James 1:27 illustrates: "Religion that God our Father accepts as pure and faultless is this: to look after orphans and widows in their distress [engagement] and to keep oneself from being polluted by the world [purity]."

Abram understood this countercultural relationship between pursuing God and engaging the people that populate this world. Genesis 12:8 reads, "From there he...pitched his tent, with Bethel on the west and Ai on the east." Oswald Chambers expands this: "Bethel is the symbol of communion with God; Ai is the symbol of the world. Abram pitched his tent between the two."[3]

As we prepare our kids to engage in the world outside our front door, we tend to polarize to extremes— to run toward purity at the expense of engaging culture, or to embrace culture at the expense of a vibrant, connected faith. The pathway to the kind of faith that seeks to find Jesus on the face of those who disagree is based solidly on the irresistibility of Jesus Christ. He is our example of engaging the culture and yet staying pure. He had dirty hands and a clean heart—something I hope to emulate.

As we value Jesus as the central part of our communities, with our family as a microcosm of biblical community, we will begin to see a winsome transition in the culture around us—an opening to the paradoxical ways of the kingdom.

These questions help us probe the issues our kids face with others. They help us focus on the kingdom of God. And they highlight the important relationships God has placed in each of our lives.

Q:

Whom do you miss the most today? What do you miss most about him or her?

Q:

Who is the biggest cheerleader or encourager in your life? Be specific: What does he or she do that encourages you?

Q:

Who is your best friend right now? Who was your best friend two years ago? What changed?

Q:

If you were to design housing for the homeless in your city or town, what would you include? A restaurant? A gym?

Q:

If I gave you $50 and told you to make some-one's day with it, what would you do?

Q:

Who is the funniest person you know? Why is he or she funny?

Q:

When was the last time you were surprised or
startled? What happened?

Q:

Who is someone you know who is hurting?
What is causing the pain? Let's pray for him or
her tonight.

Q:

When was the last time you yelled? What happened to make you holler?

Q:

What is the nicest thing someone's done for you?

Q:

What argument with a friend do you most remember? What happened?

Q:

What was the most discouraging thing that happened to you last year?

Q:

What was the best place (a hotel, campsite, friend's house…) that you've stayed?

❒

Q:

Who is your hero? (Try to choose someone who has recently lived or is alive today.) Why?

❒

Q:

Who was the hardest person to say goodbye to?

Conclusion: The End of the Conversation?

I'm one of those dinosaurs who passionately promotes the family dinner table—and the discourse it brings. Both the family meal and lively conversation seem to be lost arts these days. The other day, my daughter came home from an event where her high school teachers had several kids over for dinner. This event begged the question, "What do you do for dinner each night?"

Sophie was the *only* kid who ate with her family every night.

Friends of my kids have said things like, "I really wish we could have dinner as a family." Or "I get my own dinner." Or "We never eat dinner together." They say this with a wistfulness, a longing.

I understand our crazy culture of do-do-do, go-go-go. I am fully entrenched in it. But the rewards of prioritizing time together far outweigh anything we could accomplish outside the family circle.

Which is why I was thrilled when I heard the former editor of *Gourmet* magazine, Ruth Reichl, talk about her best practices. She said she was so thankful she went back to creating a family dinner every night. She talked about the beauty of eating together and of how, when you share a meal, you also get to hear the hearts of your kids.

I don't do everything right as a parent (great understatement!), but our family has done at least one thing well: We've shared a meal together every night. It grounds us. Centers us. Brings us together. I pray I've instilled that same desire with my kids so that when they grow up and have their own families, they'll be just as countercultural and dare to eat dinner together every night. Consider this from my book *You Can Raise Courageous and Confident Kids*:

> The more we value conversation and discourse, the more we cultivate discussion in our home, the better equipped our children will be. Some have called this developing our child's "emotional intelligence," helping them to be able to interact in any situation. As we engage our children, we nurture this type of intelligence, where children learn instinctively how to think about the world and how to interact with the people in it.[4]

Asking great questions and sharing life together are at the center of our family's passion. Our desire as parents is to create a home our kids brag about to their friends, a place they're wildly enthusiastic about coming home to. As you finish reading the words of this book, let me leave you with ten practical ways to foster that kind of home.

1. *Let kindness reign.* Determine to treat your children and spouse with the same sweetness you'd give a stranger you're trying to impress. Remember that God's kindness is what leads us to repentance. What makes us think anything different would evoke our children's repentance?

2. *Welcome hard questions.* Having questions is okay. You asked them, didn't you? Give your children the same freedom. Let them vent. Let them worry. Welcome their wrestling. Don't give pat answers; instead, let them work through their questions. Love them through a period of questioning.

3. *Be there.* Give your children the rare gift of your focused attention. Look into their eyes. Ask great questions. Relax alongside them. Dr. Ross Campbell says, "Focused attention

makes a child feel he is the most important person in the world in his parents' eyes."

4. *Limit media.* Steer your children away from mindless interaction with the TV or video games. Set limits and stick to them. Dare to believe your children are creative, innovative kids who can create instead of idly recreate.

5. *Play outside.* We've lost the importance of outdoor play. Even if it means walking the neighborhood with your kids, swimming alongside them in a community pool, or taking a nature hike, dare to move beyond the four walls of your home to venture out to see God's creation.

6. *Weep and rejoice at the right times.* We are to weep with those who weep and rejoice with those who rejoice (Romans 12:15). When a child has a difficult day, scoop her into your arms and cry alongside her. When she makes a great grade, jump up and down and celebrate with ice cream.

7. *Cherish childhood.* Our kids grow up so fast in this crazy culture. Keep them kids as long as you can. Let them play, run, stretch, linger. Limit activities when they're younger so

they don't become little stressed-out adults at age ten.

8. *Read together.* The most haven-producing thing I do as a mommy is simply to read to my kids. I still read to my 12-year-old! Discover books on CD as a family, lessening the tedium of car rides without popping in a DVD. My kids have stayed in the car to listen to a story finish.

9. *Laugh hard, but not at another's expense.* Joking and laughter are blessings you can add to create a fun-loving haven, but be cautious not to laugh at your kids' expense or allow them to laugh at others' expense (including yours). Watch funny, clean movies together. Tell jokes. Tell family stories over and over until they become ridiculous. A lighthearted family that doesn't take itself too seriously fosters a haven-home.

10. *Practice God's presence in the mundane.* Require chores of your kids. Such discipline teaches them important life skills. Even so, introduce joy as you work. Turn up the music, dance, laugh. By learning to practice the

presence of God during the chores of life, you create a productive, gratitude-based home.[5]

Exploring the questions in this book alongside your family will help create the haven-like home you've longed for. Even if you've struggled, even if your kids roll their eyes at probing questions, even if all your work seems to have been for naught, remember that the effort you put forth as a curious parent builds an irresistible home little by little.

Never stop asking questions. Never cease being curious about the children God has placed in your life. Seek God for kid-shaped questions in each moment and pray that He will help you parent well every day. We walk the parenting journey by His strength. We pursue our children's hearts by His intentionality. And by His love, we love them well.

Notes

1. Ivy Beckwith, *Postmodern Children's Ministry: Ministry to Children in the 21st Century* (Grand Rapids, MI: Zondervan, 2004), 136.
2. Oswald Chambers, *My Utmost for His Highest* (Westwood, NJ: Barbour, 1935), 49.
3. Chambers, *My Utmost for His Highest*, 6.
4. Adapted from my book *You Can Raise Courageous and Confident Kids* (Eugene, OR: Harvest House, 2007). Formerly titled *Authentic Parenting in a Postmodern Culture*.
5. Ibid.

If you wish to connect mom-to-mom
or woman-to-woman with Mary,
contact her at

maryedemuth@sbcglobal.net
twitter.com/MaryDeMuth
facebook.com/Mary.DeMuth
www.marydemuth.com

To learn more about Harvest House books
or to read sample chapters, log on to our website:
www.harvesthousepublishers.com

HARVEST HOUSE PUBLISHERS
EUGENE, OREGON